And Flowers for All Seasons

For my Father
who taught me that
'to everything there is a Season
and a time to every purpose'.

JANUARY

The daisy: Chaucer's favourite flower

AND FLOWERS
FOR ALL SEASONS

by
Katy Bell

BREWIN BOOKS

Published by K.A.F. Brewin Books,
Studley, Warwickshire, B80 7LX.
November 1988

Typeset in Garamond
Designed by Mike Hill Graphics, 46 Rother Street, Stratford-on-Avon
and made and printed in Great Britain by
Supaprint (Redditch) Ltd., Redditch, Worcs.

A Family Tradition

Flowers have always held a special place in history and were widely given as tokens of love, friendship or fellowship before ordinary people could read or write. But it was in Victorian times that pressed flowers became recognised as an art form, when the language of flowers under-went a great revival. Many books, mostly translated from the French language, were written about flowers and their meanings. Flowers given to a loved one were treasured and their preservation of great importance.

My Great Grandmother, Jane Worral, was born in the reign of Queen Victoria. She lived for most of her life in the tiny village of Grandborough, Warwickshire. Books passed on through the family show that she was a clever cook and a keen gardener. She raised several sons and three daughters: May, Drucilla, and Nell. Later she became Grandmother to 'little Phyllis' who was my mother. To her, Great Grandmother Jane passed on her love of the countryside and the art of pressing flowers.

Phyllis grew up and moved over the border into Northamptonshire where she met Victor Bell, a lad of Scots descent whose family lived in Welford. They were married in the early ninteen-thirties and had two daughters: Rosemary and Delphine. While Father was away fighting in the Second World War, Mother kept the girls amused in the summertime by showing them how to press flowers growing in and around Welford.

My sisters were grown up by the time I was born in the nineteen fifties and had a beautiful portfolio of pressed flowers, gathered as a record of their childhood. In my mind's eye, filled with tissue and bound in linen, I can still see their book. It inspired me as a child to gather flowers and learn how to press them and make them into pictures. A vision of nodding buttercups, walkways spangled with daisies, and my Mother's smiling face, is conjured up even as I write.

Sadly, Mother died in 1975, long before I became a professional Floral Artist. But encouraged by my Father, who grows most of the flowers I press, I have carried on the family tradition with love and pride.

I am married to Peter, we also live in Welford and have a charming little daughter, Holly Marie. Apart from Boo-Boo Bear, one of her most treasured possessions is a tiny flower press and she is surprisingly adept at pressing daisies and pansies. So, long may the family tradition continue!

Early Spring:
A picture containing violas, heartsease,
daisies, wallflower buds, rock rose buds,
celandines, forget-me-nots, rock rose
flowers, and cow parsley leaves.

AND FLOWERS FOR ALL SEASONS

Contents

January brings the snow

JANUARY

Makes our feet and fingers glow

January Flowers

	meaning
Daisy	Practical beauty. Innocence
Winter aconite	Misanthropy
Erica	Change
Forsythia	Grace

Birthflower	Daisy

Birthstone	Garnet. From the Latin for pomegranite whose seeds it resembles.

Family sayings:

'New beginnings with a New Year'.

'Off with the Old and on with the New'.

'Make new friends but keep the old
one is silver, the other gold'.

Diary Notes for January

January 1st, Happy New Year!

I drew back the curtains with a flourish this morning to reveal a clear, frosty start to the year. Definitely a day for early country walking to work up an appetite for lunch. Peter and I decided to take Holly, our small daughter for a brisk walk along Hall Lane. We could not follow the bridle road all the way to Kilworth because she wanted to show off her new bicycle. The road only lasts for the first mile or so, and then recedes to a cart track unsuitable for vehicles. It was still very cold when we set out. Holly managed to fall off her bicycle twice, howling loudly each time and causing the flocks of sparrows resting in the trees to take to the air in alarm.

Walking along I noticed amongst all the dead greenery of last year, a few clumps of cow parsley struggling up through the hard ground. There was also plenty of ground ivy, but it goes rather dull in Winter. In years gone by the thick stems of the ivy were fashioned into cups from which children drank their milk to ward off whooping cough.

Further along the lane there is a pond. Last year's reedmace still stood starkly around the edge, the reed heads looking like patient sentries waiting for Spring.

January 3rd

Above average temperatures for the time of year! 'a weather breeder' meaning bad weather to come. Peter has gone back to work so Holly and I spent an hour on the garden this afternoon, tidying up. We have a few winter-flowering heathers making a pretty show of pink on the rockery. I also found one brave little daisy, (Chaucer's favourite flower) blooming on the lawn. It had red tips to its petals. I find only the early daisies have these. By July, the petals are usually all white and the flowers do not press well.

The greenhouse is almost empty except for one last box of pansies to be transferred to my flower press later in the week. Next month Father will transfer tray upon tray of seedlings from his greenhouse to mine. These will later make up my stock of pressed flowers for the year.

January 6th

Twelfth night. All Christmas decorations must be taken down before midnight.

Janaury 8th

Deep, deep snow. Holly was beside herself with delight and rushed out to build a snowman. There was much giggling and laughing and a very fine snowman was created in the end. I cleared the pathways to our house. Looking across at the shrubbery I thought how beautiful the *viburnum opulus* looked, its clusters of dark red berries enfolded in snow. The garden birds do not care for the berries, preferring the deep red bags of peanuts I buy from the village shop. However, this evening I saw a mistle thrush sitting on one of the branches. These birds are fond of all kinds of berries. There is hope for the viburnum yet.

January 14th

It is still bitterly cold. I spent the day sitting by a log fire and planning my Crafts Calendar for the year. I have decided to organise a show of my work on May Day Monday in Newtown Linford. I have also booked stands at both the Northampton Show and the Town and Country Show, Stoneleigh in addition to stands at a number of crafts fairs and in and around Leicestershire, Nottinghamshire and of course, my home county, Northamptonshire. I just hope I shall be able to pick and press enough flowers and foliage to last the year. Even in January there are usually a few primroses, snowdrops, and winter aconite in bloom and many young leaves to press too. But it has been so cold with daytime temperatures barely reaching freezing point, that I have not ventured out to look for specimens yet.

January 23rd

The frosty weather is still with us. This afternoon there was a hail storm. The stones danced and clattered down for ages and were the size of marrowfat peas.

January 26th

It is still very cold. On the way to church this morning, I was surprised to see that many of Thursday's hailstones are still scattered in the ditches and hedgerows. Let us hope things improve in February.

January Recipes

Katy's answer to those Winter Chills:

Claret Cup: Great Grandma's recipe

      1 bottle Claret

      1 bottle soda water

      4 tablespoons of caster sugar

      ¼ teaspoonful of grated nutmet

      1 liqueur glass of maraschino

      a sprig of green borage

      1½lbs pounded ice

Put all the ingredients into a silver cup, regulating the ice according to the weather. If very warm a large quantity would be necessary. On cold winter days the Cup may be served mulled. Hand round the Cup with a clean napkin passed through one of the handles so that it may be wiped after each guest has partaken thereof.

Cough Mixture: (also taken from Great Grandma's recipe book)

      22 drops of oil of aniseed

      12 drops of oil of peppermint

      ½oz Spanish Liquorice

      ½oz salts of tartar

All the above to be dissolved in one pint of boiling water. Take a tablespoonful when the cough is troublesome.

Flecknoe Fizz: Grandma's recipe book.

Chop up a large Spanish onion. Put it in a large screw top jar with a cup full of brown sugar and half-a-pint of malt vinegar.

After it has stood or a few hours, stir it all up and take a dessertspoonful of the juice 3 or 4 times a day, particularly before you go out.

Flecknoe is a tiny village in Warwickshire. Grandma lived there for some years after her marriage. My mother was born there on 28th November 1915. The snow was so heavy that day it broke down the old apple tree in the garden. My Grandfather chopped it up to provide warmth for the newborn baby, Phyllis May.

I think Flecknoe Fizz is a remedy of prevention rather than cure. One's breath would smell so strongly it would prevent others from getting close enough to pass on their germs!

FEBRUARY

*Heartsease, forget-me-nots, and snowdrops,
who 'bringeth Hope and Spring'.*

February brings the rain

FEBRUARY

Thaws the frozen lake again

February Flowers

	meaning
Bellis perennis	Beauty
Anemone	Forsaken
Crocus	Youthful Gladness
Jonquillia	I desire a return of affection
Hyacinth	Constancy
Polyanthus	Pride of riches
Snowdrop	Hope

Birthflower   Snowdrop

Birthstone   Amethyst. From the Greek word meaning "not drunken". The stone according to legend inspires fairness and a sense of duty.

Family sayings:

'The snowdrop bringeth Hope and Spring'.

'We journey through this World but once
and have short time to stay
Whatever good we mean to do
Had best be done today.
For such another golden chance
We may await in vain,
Now is the time, because
We shall not pass this way again'.

Uncle Chub's Grace:

'We will thank the Lord for what we have had,
If we had some more we should have been glad,
But as the times they are so bad,
We will thank the Lord for what we have had'.

Diary Notes for February

February 1st.

'February fill dyke, black or white'. Black this time – it is raining.

February 2nd. Feast Day: Purification of St. Mary

The feast day is no longer celebrated locally, but in years gone by it was the tradition for young girls to pick bunches of snowdrops and wear them as a sign of purity.

It has been too cold for the snowdrops to bloom in the garden, although we have some in bud in a sheltered spot by the wall.

February 3rd

Holly and I were surprised to find a hen pheasant scratching for food in Mr. Bott's orderly garden on the corner of Wakefield Drive, this morning. I have never seen a pheasant in the village before although there are plenty in the woods which surround the village. They usually feed on wild fruits, seeds and leaves and are partial to the flowers of the wood anemone, as well as insects and worms.

February 9th

We have had several falls of snow which the wind has whipped into deep drifts across the hedgerows and local roads. However I braved the Husbands Bosworth road, (which is exposed for miles and is always snowbound at least once a year) to do my shopping in Market Harborough. I could not resist buying an armful of daffodils, narcissus, and jonquillia to brighten up the house. I expect they will also end up in my flower press.

Jonquillia press extremely well and look pretty on Springtime pictures. I have also ordered a bundle of wattle (Acacia) which make interesting little "buttons" when pressed.

February 11th, Shrove Tuesday

Father came to lunch today. Pancakes were served just the way he likes them, with caster sugar and freshly squeezed orange juice.

By tradition pancakes were a way of using up eggs before the fast of Lent which starts on Ash Wednesday. Eggs are the ancient Egyptian symbol of rebirth and were forbidden during Lent.

February 14th, St. Valentine's Day

I received a beautiful bouquet of red roses from Peter. The rose is given as a token of love although some varieties and colours have a variation on this theme.

February 17th

I have been told the Aurora Borealis has been visible here for the first time in many years. So I talked Delphine into walking along Hall Lane to Mr. Deacon's field this evening, to wait for the phenomenon to occur. Looking rather like Flanagan and Allen in our old furry coats we picked our way through the packed ice and drifts to the field. In the distance I could hear a farm dog howling. It was bitterly cold! Looking up though we saw pale streaks of pink and golden light in the black starry sky. At first I thought they might be the lights of Leicester but Delphine pointed these out further along on the right. I decided to take her word for it and we headed for home. Her sense of direction is much better than mine, except for the occasion when she navigated us into an abattoir's car park in Loughborough on the way to a Craft Fair some years ago. But that is another story.

My father told me later that the Northern Lights can only be seen this far south during very clear conditions. They herald extremely cold weather to come and were seen here regularly in 1947.

February 18th

There was much commotion in the garden this morning. I looked out to see a barn owl feasting on a piece of bacon fat hung over Holly's swing for our more usual garden birds. He must have been desperately hungry to be hunting in daylight, but even the daytime temperature has been well below freezing point for the last few days. The starlings were disgusted with the owl for taking their breakfast and sat in a line along the wall chirping noisily. Eventually, their squawking awoke Jack, our rather care-worn black-and-white cat, who decided reluctantly to leave his spot in front of the fire to investigate. He peered through the lace curtains at the french door then gave an excellent impression of a moggy with a weak heart before creeping away to hide behind the settee.

The barn owl population is undergoing a fast decline. Their natural habitat, old barns and hollow trees have largely disappeared thanks to E.E.C. policies of taking maximum land for crop cultivation. I am sure I read somewhere that the barn owls number only one-thousand-five-hundred at present.

February 21st

No sign of the cold weather loosening its grip. At this time of the year I am usually picking the first heartease and primroses for pressing. Violets have also been known to bloom in February.

In Father's greenhouse however, Spring has firmly been declared. Tiny seedlings are germinating by the tray full. We should have a good crop of godetia, taggets, salvias, pansies, verbena and candytuft to keep my flower presses bulging.

We have decided to keep all the seedlings in one greenhouse for the time being. The extremes in temperature make it difficult for us to keep even one greenhouse constantly warm.

February 28th

The snow is still with us. It has been the coldest February for over forty years.

February Recipe

Love Cake
Great Grandma's recipe book.

1 breakfast cup full of flour, and one of sugar, a little butter well rubbed into the flour, 2 teaspoonful of baking powder, 2 eggs and a little milk. Beat all up well with a fork, not very stiff. Bake them in a buttered tin, hot oven, for about 20 minutes.

The Language of Roses

(hand written book very old)

Roses are given as a token of Love:

	meaning
Rose: Austrian	Thou art all that is lovely
Rose, Boule de Neige	Only for thee
Rose, Bridal	Happy love
Rose, Burgundy	Unconscious beauty
Rose, Cabbage	Ambassador of love
Rose, Campion	Only deserve my love
Rose, Carolina	Love is dangerous
Rose, Charles le fievree	Speak low if you speak of love
Rose, China	Beauty always new
Rose, Christmas	Relieve my anxiety
Rose, Daily	I aspire to your smile
Rose, Damask	Brilliant complexion
Rose, Deep red	Bashful
Rose, Dog	Pleasure and pain
Rose, Gloire de Dejon	Messenger of love
Rose, Guelder	Age
Rose, Hundred leaved	Pride
Rose, Japan	Beauty is your only attraction
Rose, Hopper	Encouragement
Rose, La France	A meeting by moonlight
Rose, Maiden blush	Do you love me
Rose, Monteflora	Grace
Rose, Mundi	Variety
Rose, Musk	Capricious
Rose, Musk, cluster	Charm
Rose, Nephitos	Infatuation
Rose, Single	Simplicity
Rose, Thornless	Early attachment
Rose, Unique	Do not say I am beautiful
Rose, White	I am worthy of you
Rose, White (wilting)	Passing fancy
Rose, Yellow	Jealousy
Rose, York or Lancaster	War
Rose, Mature placed over to buds	Secrecy
Rose, White and red together	Unity

Great Grandma's Golden Rules for Pressing Flowers

1) Never pick flowers on a dull day or after rain during the day. Flowers generally hold a great deal of hidden moisture which will result in discoloration and even moulding.

2) Only pick flowers after mid-day on a sunny day, so that the dew has evaporated. Usually by mid-day the flowers are fully open.

3) Where possible leave flowers whole.

4) Pinch petals into place – especially daisies – and place face down on pressing tissue.

5) Do not press flowers onto blotting paper. Great Grandma used tissue paper. However, I find this gives an unnatural shiny finish. Good quality toilet tissue is best.

6) Use a proper flower press so that pressure is evenly distributed. Sheets of newspaper may also be placed between the cardboard sheets to help absorb moisture more readily.

7) Place flower press in a warm, dry atmosphere. My presses are kept at a controlled temperature of 70F. An airing cupboard is ideal for small presses.

8) Label layers so that the tabs are visible from the outside.

9) Keep flowers in the press for at least six weeks. No peeping!

10) Pressed flowers should be stored between their layers of tissue to keep them flat and in good condition. Larkspur, nemesia, and rock roses are particularly delicate when pressed and should be handled as little as possible.

MARCH:

An assortment of Spring flowers

March brings breezes sharp and chill

MARCH

Shakes the dancing daffodil

March Flowers

	meaning
Celandine	Joy to come
Sweet violet	Modesty
Daffodil	Chivalry
Forget-me-not	True love
Pansy	Thoughts
Primrose	Early youth
Heartease	You occupy my thoughts

Birthflower	Sweet violet

Birthstone   Aquamarine. Derived from sea water it is said to be the spirit of hope and a promise of good things to come.

Family sayings:

'The kiss of the sun for pardon,
The songs of the birds for mirth,
One is nearer God's heart in a garden,
Than anywhere else on earth'.

'If along Life's pathway,
You by chance should see
A tiny Forget-me-not,
Pick it and think of me'.

Diary Notes for March

March 1st, St. David's Day

The traditional emblem of the Welsh people is the leek. During the Welsh wars, soldiers marching across fields of the vegetable picked some and stuck them in their hats. They won the battle and so the leek became their mascot. The Welsh Guards still use the leek as their insignia on St. David's Day.

In 1911, at the investiture of Edward, Prince of Wales, the daffodil was adopted as the emblem of Wales. It means chivalry. Shakespeare wrote that daffodils 'Come before the swallow dares, and take the winds of March with beauty'.

March 10th

I decided to look for celandines today. They are usually one of the earliest flowers to bloom, but favour shady woodland areas. I was delighted to find some buds in the hedgerows round and about. I suspect that the continued frosty weather will keep them in bud for a long time to come. They only bloom when the sun shines.

March 13th

Visited a few old haunts in Warwickshire with Uncle Fred and Aunt Jean who are on holiday here from Scotland. Despite the cold we went first to Grandborough, to show Holly the house where Uncle and my Mother lived as children and also the little church where they attended Sunday School. With much pride Uncle pointed out the pew he had sat in whilst a choir boy. He later graduated to pumping the organ! The church clock chimed the hour just as we were leaving. The bell still has the rusty sound I well remember from childhood visits to my Grandparents' house.

On the way home we stopped again so that Holly could admire new born lambs in a paddock.

It is foggy this evening. 'Fogs in March, frosts in May'.

March 15th

The weather is warmer today and the daffodils and tulips in the garden are shaking out their dancing skirts at last. Winter aconites are bravely showing their delicate yellow faces to the sun.

There are not many wild flowers around but the celandines are busy making a carpet of lemon in the woods.

March 16th

Out walking, Holly and I found a huge patch of sweet violets. They are not such a common Spring flower now, various methods of hedging and ditching have ruined their natural habitat. Father has some growing in his garden. The plants were transported from Grandborough years ago. Only the sweet violet is scented and was a favourite of Queen Victoria.

March 17th, St. Patrick's Day

The emblem of Ireland is the shamrock. St. Patrick is said to have used the trifoliate leaves of the plant to illustrate the Holy Trinity.

March 21st

First day of Spring.

March 24th

March many weathers indeed! Gale force winds have wreaked havoc across the countryside damaging property and up-rooting trees. It was not quite so bad here, but I lost most of the glass from the greenhouse.

March 30th

Forget-me-nots and heartease blooming well in Dad's greenhouse. I will pick them for my flower presses soon. Spring flowers are very fragile and often garden blooms become damaged by the wind and rain. We cultivate a good number behind glass as my pictures look better if the flowers are in perfect condition.

March Recipes

*All from Grandma's recipe book hand written
and well-thumbed, dated 1908.*

'Jugged Hare' —Time four hours.

A hare, a small onion, a lemon, two glasses of port wine, a tablespoonful of mushroom ketchup, five cloves, pepper, salt, a little cayenne, butter and flour.

Late Spring:
A picture containing delphiniums, rock roses,
buttercups, violas, wall flowers and grasses.

Mode:

Skin the hare and cut it into pieces but do not wash it. Dredge it with flour, and fry it a nice golden brown in butter, seasoning it with a little salt and pepper and cayenne. Make about a pint-and-a-half of gravy from the beef. Put the pieces of hare into a jar, add the onion stock with the cloves, the lemon peeled and cut and pour in the gravy. Cover the jar closely to keep in the steam, put into a stewpan of cold water and let it boil for four hours. If a young hare, three hours will be sufficient. When done add a teaspoonful of ketchup, two glasses of port wine, and a piece of butter rolled in flour, and with some fried forcemeat balls. Serve with red currant jelly.

Parsnip Wine. March is the month for this.

    4lbs parsnips
    3lbs sugar
    3 oranges and 2 lemons
    1 gallon water

Mode:

Wash parsnips, weigh them and put them into a clean white bag or muslin. Bring water to the boil, put in the parsnips and boil until tender. Take out. Peel oranges, and cut off white skin then slice. Cut lemons in the same way and add to boiling water with three pieces of root ginger and the sugar. Boil for half an hour then put all into a clean earthenware jar to cool. When just warm put in one tablespoon of Balm or yeast and let it ferment for twelve hours or more. Skim off the yeast and strain into a clean jar leaving cork loose until it has stopped fermenting. Tighten up the corks and let stand for six months or more then bottle.

Hair dressing.

    3oz spirits of Mormary
    ½oz sweet oil of almonds
    1 dram essence of lemon
    ½oz spirit of ammonia

Mix all thoroughly together.

April brings the primrose sweet

APRIL

Scatters daisies at our Feet

APRIL

King cups, daisies, and limanthes make up
this pretty design

April Flowers

	meaning
Bluebell	Constancy
Flowering currant	You please all
Marsh marigold	Desire of riches
Cowslip	Winning grace
Tulip, red	Declaration of love
Tulip, yellow	Hopeless love
Tulip, variegated	Beautiful eyes
Dog violet	Faithfulness

Birthflower   Marsh marigold

Birthstone   Diamond. The word is taken from 'Adamas' meaning indomitable. It protects the wearer from evil and sickness.

Family sayings:

'April showers bring May flowers'.

'The primrose on the woodlands lee
Is more than gold or lands to me'.

'O to be in England
Now that April's here!'.

A song taught to Grandma in School about 85 years ago.

'Will you buy my pretty flowers,
I toiled full hard for them,
And sweeter blooms never grew,
Upon the parent stem.

Sweet primrose and violets
And daffodils have I,
And bluebells fair that scent the air
As passing breezes fly'.

Diary Notes for April

April 7th

'O to be in England' Now that Winter's here . . . more snow showers today. It is still cold but the garden flowers are managing to survive.

April 11th

Gathered flowering currant leaves and florets for my press this afternoon. The tiny red flowers should be pressed individually for the best results. Forget-me-nots are in bloom in the garden too. I press them on the stem, taking off the very tight buds at the top of the stalk before placing them on the tissue.

April 19th, Primrose Day

Today was named in memory of Disraeli. His favourite flower was the primrose. My Great Grandfather, John Bell, was his coachman.

The continued poor weather has kept the primroses in bud here, although when I visited Aunt Drue a few weeks ago the primroses in her garden were blooming in profusion.

Cowslips, a member of the same family are also to be found in the hedgerows at this time of year. Last year I bought a packet of cowslip seeds. But, I only have one plant to show for my labours. This wild flower is obviously very temperamental. Any found growing in the countryside should be left in peace.

April 23rd, St. George's Day

The red rose is the traditional flower of the English and a rosebud is worn on the coat lapels of the City gents today.

April 24th

Walking to our local reservoir I came across a large patch of king cups sometimes called marsh marigolds. They prefer marshy land or damp woodlands and flower from March to September. The name 'king cup' is taken from an old English word 'cop' for the shiny buttons a king would wear on his coat.

April 25th

There was a programme about spiders on the Radio today. It is said that spiders are making extra-large webs this year to combat a poor summer.

April 29th

Taking the 'B' road from Sibbertoft through Marston Trussell to Market Harborough I noticed the fields beyond Coombe's Hill are carpeted with bluebells once more. I think Spring has finally crept up on us.

Bluebells were used in the manufacture of glue in the 16th century. Nowadays, this pretty English flower is under protection. Evidence suggests though, that more harm is done by walkers trampling on the leaves, cutting off the plant's food supply, than by picking the flowers.

April 30th

The swallows have arrived to view their nesting sites under the eaves of our house. Before the house was built a mud and wattle wall stood on the site and this was a nesting area for the swallows for generations.

We always have two families of swallows on one side of the house and a family of housemartins on the other, which is nearly always in shade.

April Recipes

Cowslip Tea for Giddiness and Nervous Excitement
May Lane's recipe.

One pound of freshly gathered flowers, infused in a pint-and-half of boiling water. Add sugar to taste. If simmered down to a thick syrup and taken at bed time, it will be sure to induce good sound slumber.

Rhubarb Beer

Grandma's recipe book.

This beer is best made with field grown rhubarb.

1lb of demerara sugar to each gallon of water.
4lbs rhubarb
A little yeast or a tablespoonful of Brewer's Balm.

Mode:

Wash but do not peel the rhubarb, put it into a large unglazed earthenware pan or wooden tub, and bruise thoroughly with a wooden mallet or a rolling pin.

Add the sugar and pour on the boiling water.

Stir until the sugar has dissolved and while the liquor is still warm stir in the yeast or balm. If liked add ½oz of bruised ginger root. Let it all stand for twenty-four hours covered with a cloth.

Strain and bottle but do not cork the bottles tightly for two or three days. One ounce of yeast only, should be used for three to four gallons of beer. It should be put with a teaspoonful of sugar into a teacup and mixed until it liquifies. Then half fill the cup with warm water and stand in a basin of water of the same temperature. In eight to ten minutes it will be all froth and ready for use.

This bottled beer will be ready for use in a week but will be better for standing a little longer.

May brings flocks of pretty lambs

MAY

Skipping by their fleecy dames

MAY:

Pansies and buttercups

May Flowers

	meaning
Cow parsley	Inspiration
Wallflower	Fidelity in adversity
Lily-of-the-valley	Return of happiness
Hawthorn	Hope
Lilac	Humility
Apple blossom	Preference
Delphinium	Haughtiness
Rock rose	Quiet affection
Buttercup	Ingratitude
Herb Robert	Wit

Birthflower	Lily-of-the-valley
Birthstone	Emerald. Dedicated to Venus, this stone is said to protect the wearer from drowning.

Family sayings:

'Life is mainly froth and bubble,
Two things stand like stones,
Kindness in another's trouble
Courage in your own'.

'When apple trees bloom well in May
You can eat apples night and day'.

29

Diary Notes for May

May 1st

I noticed on the way to Rugby, a swan's nest very high up on the bank of the reservoir. This is supposed to signify a wet Summer. There are three species of swan to be found in the British Isles but two are Winter visitors only: the Whopper Swan and Bewick Swan. The third species is the Mute Swan and I think this is the species to be found on the reservoir. It lays between five and seven eggs, grey green in colour. Incubation is about five weeks.

Pliny the elder in his book "Natural History" written over one thousand years ago, states that the normally silent Mute Swans 'before their death, sing most sweetly'. This untrue statement led to the originaion of the 'swan song' and many legends regarding swans and death.

May 2nd – own show Newtown Linford

I had worked hard to produce enough pictures and decorative items to fill the Sunday School building, which is situated near the park. The show took the theme "The Flowers and the Children" and was intended to be a May Day celebration of Floral Art.

May 6th

The cow parsley, known as M'Lady's Lace in these parts is blooming at last and the roadsides look like long ribbons of lace with this pretty plant bobbing and swaying in the breeze. The flowers are pretty when pressed and are popular on my pictures.

May 10th

A lovely blustery Spring day, with gentle clouds scudding across the blue sky, little lambs dancing in the fields, and the air alive with bird-song.

I spent the afternoon – from five minutes past twelve as Great Gran' suggested in her 'Golden Rules' gathering and pressing flowers. An afternoon's labour resulted in a press filled with daisies, buttercups, wallflowers, forget-me-nots, alyssum (red from the greenhouse) and primroses. I also gathered many pretty leaves including Herb Robert a wild plant whose stems and leaves turn red in Autumn.

May 16th

The hawthorn is in bloom brightening up the hedgerows this sunny day. Although it was given as a sign of protection against evil in the Middle Ages, it is now considered unlucky to bring it indoors.

May 17th, Moulton Festival

This year's rather wet celebration of Spring complete with Morris dancers and the crowning of the May Queen is one of my favourite shows. I usually talk Delphine, my long suffering sister, into acting as sales lady for my stand in the Crafts marquee while Holly and I disappear into the crowd to watch the Ceremony.

Just before 10 a.m. the crowd gathers in the village Public Gardens in hushed anticipation of the May Maiden's arrival. The music and ringing of tiny bells on the Morris men's feet can be heard long before her chariot comes into view.

The chariot bedecked with garlands of lilac, hawthorn and many different sweet scented flowers is pulled along by pairs of dancing Morris men. These are preceded by pairs dancing and carrying hooped garlands of spring flowers. Further pairs follow the chariot and a company of accordian, drum and flute players, complete the procession.

To applause from the crowd the May Maiden steps from her chariot, up the steps and onto the flower-bedecked throne where she is crowned by last year's May Queen. The new Queen then declares the festival open and dancing displays from Morris men from all over the country begin and continue at intervals throughout the day.

May 20th

At 'My Way' Dad's house, a recently constructed nesting box placed in the garden has been occupied by a pair of 'Black Caps'. Being a wise gardener, Father hopes that the insect population will be kept under control once the brood is hatched and feeding starts. A single pair of great tits will need up to seven thousand insects to feed their young.

May 26th, Holdenby House Crafts Show.

Between the car park and the outbuildings where the fair is

held there is a beautiful wooded area where bush vetch, red campion and bugloss (a type of forget-me-not) grow in tangled profusion along with cow parsley, daisies, buttercups and grasses. The crafts village is set up in the outbuildings of the house and many traditional crafts such as spinning, and the making of horseshoes are demonstrated.

May 30th

The delphiniums are in flower. We have some pretty blue ones in our garden. The leaves of the plant are supposed to be poisonous and in years gone by were used as an insect repellent.

I also have a patch of lily-of-the-valley in bloom, by our back gate. I bought the plants last year and now have a show of white scented flowers as a reward.

May Recipes

Milk Jelly

(Grandma's delicious recipe and a favourite of mine when I visit her)

1 pint milk, less two tablespoons
2 tablespoons water
1 packet jelly

Mode:

Melt the jelly with two tablespoons of water over the fire but do not allow to boil. Remove from the fire and add the cold milk slowly. This causes the milk to curdle slowly. Pour the mixture into a wetted mould and leave to set. Turn into a glass dish and decorate with cream if desired. When turned out the lower part of the jelly will be solid and the top clear.

Chocolate Cake

My recipe – a firm favourite with Holly!

8oz caster sugar
8oz soft margarine
4 eggs
7oz self-raising flower and 1oz cocoa mixed together
1 tablespoon warm water.

Mode:

Cream sugar and margarine until smooth. Whisk eggs and beat one tablespoon into the mixture at a time. Add the flour and one tablespoon of warm water. Divide mixture between two greased 7 inch baking tins. Bake 375F for 25 minutes until firm to the touch. Turn out of tins immediately.

When the sponges are cold sandwich together using butter cream filling made with: 3oz butter or creaming margarine, 4oz icing sugar, 2oz cocoa powder, 1 teaspoon warm water. Sieve icing sugar and cocoa powder and cream together with the butter then add the warm water for a softer mixture.

Strawberry Custard Pie – Grandma's recipe

Line a pie dish with short crust pastry and bake it till golden brown. Put into it a pint of fresh strawberries and cover them with half a cupful of sugar. Make a thick custard and whilst still hot pour it over the fruit. Allow to cool before serving.

JUNE
THE last of the wallflowers and the first
of the larkspur make up these pictures

June brings tulips lilies roses

JUNE

Fills the children's hands with posies

June Flowers

	meaning
Dog rose	Pleasure and pain
Foxglove	Insincerity
Herb bennett	Child like
Lady's mantle	War
Bramble	Envy
Honeysuckle	Bonds of love
Nemesia	Laughter
Godetia	Will you dance with me
Lobelia	Malevolence
Coral bells (Heuchera)	Wedded bliss
Larkspur	Haughtiness

Birthflower   Dog rose

Birthstone   Pearl. The emblem of the noble and ensures faithfulness of a loved one if worn next to the heart.

Family sayings:

'Gather ye Rosebuds while ye may
Old time is still a flying
And this same flower that smiles today
Tomorrow will be dying'.

'One swallow does not make a summer'.

'And in the month of June
The cuckoo changes tune'.

Diary Notes for June

June 1st

Much activity in Father's bird house . . . the wee birds have hatched. Holly is convinced it is Elfin work that lets the birds out of the eggs.

June 11th

Despite the weather being much warmer recently, today for a change we have had a hailstorm. There has also been a flurry of snow in the Grampians.

June 13th (It is a Friday too – lucky for some)

There was only one swan on the reservoir today. I still do not know if there are any young ones yet.

June 15th, Fathers' Day

It has been really hot today – 85 degrees F. I started the day by going to church with Holly. All the church windows were open and just before the service started, it was fascinating to watch the dappled sunlight through the evergreens as I sat in my usual pew.

Later in the day I filled another press with flowers and foliage. The dog roses are blooming in abundance in the hedgerows. But I have several bushes in the garden, so I do not need to scramble in the countryside to gather a supply. If pressing them: remove the seedbox from behind the flower-head first and then press the whole flower face-down on the tissue. Other types of rose are rather tedious as all the petals should be removed from the stem and pressed individually. The flower then has to be reconstructed for placing on a picture.

June 16th

On the way into Market Harborough this morning, I spied a huge patch of daisies on the green at Lubenham. I decided to hurry through my shopping list and make time to pick some on the way home. But by the time I returned, 'one man and his dog' had cleared the whole of the green with a large lawn-mower. What a great pity that the daisy 'embroiderer of the carpet earth' is so ruthlessly treated!

June 17th

There are glow worms in the Old Woodhouse Wood. One is very lucky these days to observe them.

June 18th

In the cool of the evening the baby Black Caps left their home in Dad's nesting box. There were six young – but only five flew away into the sunset; the tiniest had been trampled by its sturdier peers.

June 21st. Longest Day.

June 24th, Midsummer Day.

Peter, Holly and I went walking in the woods this evening. Holly collected a few fir cones to make a Christmas table decoration. The foxgloves are just coming into full bloom. The flowers do not press, indeed I understand the whole plant is poisonous. On the brighter side, it does contain the drug 'Digitalis' discovered in 1785 by William Withering for the treatment of heart disease.

Bracken fronds also carpet the woodlands at this time of the year. My Dad-in-law has a large patch at the top of his garden, which backs onto farmland, I gather my supply there.

June 27th

The godetia is in flower also its close neighbour the clarkia.

The nemesia has also bloomed well this year, but is rarely seen in my garden as I gather the flowers for my press. Nemesia should be cut back after first flowering and a second crop will result later.

I had a telephone call from my friend Sue this evening. She has completed a flower press solely of larkspur. She grows the plants in her greenhouse for me, so that they are not damaged by wind and rain.

June 28th

I saw both swans on the reservoir today and I was pleased to see they have two delightful little signets.

June 30th

The nasturtiums are coming into flower. It is said the flowers give off sparks as they have a high phosphoric acid level. The plant is rich in vitamin C and was used in the treatment of scurvy in days gone by. The leaves were also popular in salads though it has since been replaced by watercress which is a member of the same family.

June Recipes

Curds and Whey. Great Grandma's notes.

A very small piece of rennet, half a gallon of milk. Procure from the butcher a small piece of rennet, which is the stomach of the calf taken as soon as it is killed, scoured and well rubbed with salt and stretched on sticks to dry. Pour some boiling water on the rennet and let it remain for six hours, then use the liquid to turn the milk.

The milk should be warm and fresh from the cow, if allowed to cool it must be heated till it is of a degree quite equal to new milk, but do not let it get too hot. About a tablespoonful or more of rennet liquid would be sufficient to turn the milk in curds and whey. Whilst the milk is turning let it be kept in rather a warm place. From two to three hours should be sufficient to turn the milk.

Freckle Cure

Mix together:
1 tablespoonful of lemon juice
3 tablespoonful of rosewater
quarter of a drachm of pounded borax

Put all in a bottle and shake well. In four days time strain through a muslin, and dab on lotion with a sponge every night, letting it dry on.

JULY
A summer posy of larkspur, buttercups,
and limanthes

Hot July brings thundershowers

JULY

Apricots and gilly-flowers

July Flowers

	meaning
Rose	True love
Clover, red	Industry
Clover, white	Think of me
Vetch	Shyness
Poppy	Fantastic extravagance
Meadow rue	Disdain
Phlox dromundi	Unanimity
Corn marigold	Grief
Dandelion	Oracle
Burdock	Touch me not
Woody nightshade	Falsehood
Candytuft	Indifference
Meadowsweet	Neglected beauty

Birthflower	Red clover
Birthstone	Ruby. Thought to ensure a long and happy life.

Family sayings:

> 'When you hear the bluebottle hum
> You will know that summer has really come'.

Dripping for Roses – from an old recipe book

Dripping n   needed in the kitchen should be dug well in the earth round Rose bushes poor in health. This will give New Life and Radiance to   ie Old Rose bushes.

42

Early Summer:
Flowers: Dog roses, phlox, dog daisies, blue
larkspur, candytuft, and rosebuds. The leaves
are meadow rue.

Diary Notes for July

July 6th, Bosworth Show

It has been cool and bright today after a great deal of rain during the last few days. Driving towards Market Bosworth this morning I noticed that the fields of corn are starting to ripen. Many were festooned with bright red poppies. Although the flowers only last a day, each plant is capable of producing hundreds of flowers in its lifetime. The flowers turn mauve when pressed but are really too delicate to use.

July 9th

We arrived in Newcastle today to visit friends and see a concert. Driving along the motorway, Holly pointed out elder flowers still in bloom and the first florets of rosebay willow herb just peeping through. The countryside further north seems far behind our own. The corn is still very green.

July 10th

We drove home again today taking a pretty route across the fells and moors. The fells were covered with foxgloves, and the moorlands in bracken. When we stopped for lunch I also saw a giant hogweed. Its flower heads were at least eighteen inches wide and the whole plant towered six feet above my head. In years gone by the young leaves of this plant were considered a delicacy. Once boiled the taste resembles asparagus. However, it is not a good idea to handle this plant because it contains substances which cause blistering of the skin. It is definitely not a plant for the flower press!

July 15th

It has been a glorious summer day. From the garden I picked potentilla, larkspur, candytuft and the leaves of the meadow rue for my presses. The clover is in full bloom along the waysides so the bumblebees are having a wonderful time collecting nectar.

July 17th, Scotland

Away to the hills and the land of my forefathers. Delphine, Holly and I took to the motorway early this morning to avoid the traffic jams around Birmingham. I am booked to do a three day Crafts Show in Scotland this weekend at Irvine, which is only thirty miles away from where Grandmother lives.

I decided to take the A75 to Kilmarnock, Annan, and Dumfries once over the border. Just past Dumfries we toured through the pinewoods. There had just been (yet another) slight shower of rain and the air smelled fresh and resinous. Many fir cones littered the ground but to Holly's disappointment we had not enough time to stop and gather some.

We arrived in Irvine in torrential rain coupled with gale-force winds. We quickly found the site of the Crafts Show but decided to wait until "the morrow" before setting-up. Pressed flowers do not like a damp atmosphere – not to mention we three human beings!

We piled back into the car then headed for Grandma's lovely warm apartment for hot tea, homemade cakes, and sandwiches.

July 19th

We set up the Show this morning; but disaster struck at 11 a.m. when another heavy rain storm finally proved too much for the roof of the marquee and it split – duly drenching my most spectacular picture (dog roses, rock roses and larkspur set in a very ornate gold frame) and my entire stock of trinket bowls.

However, the "regulars" on the circuit soon rallied round and we are now sharing space with a goldsmith and his dog in a nice dry spot in the marquee.

July 20th

A much better day both in atmospheric conditions and 'trade winds'. The sun has been shining all day and the Scots people liked my work. What more could I ask! A stray piper even ventured into the crafts arena this afternoon and the skirl of the bagpipes soon echoed across the glen. Home tomorrow though, and on to the Northampton Show next weekend.

July 25th, Northampton Show

This is my favourite amongst the summer shows, not just because it is held on home ground but because it's a something-for-everyone kind of show. Catering for all the family, aspects of country life as diverse as wine making and floral art are on display.

So, if you like a fun packed weekend: Northampton Show is the place to be. Dearest to my heart, apart from the Fuchsia Society's tent, is the Crafts Tent. However, I must have had a mean streak when ordering my space this year. I only booked a single stand. Setting up was quite a feat yesterday, rather along the lines of 'how do you get eighteen people in a Mini car?' With great difficulty!

July Recipes

Both from Great Grandma's recipe book.

Greengage Jam

To every lb of fruit, weighed before being stoned, allow ¾lb of lump sugar. Bring fruit to a boil, then add the sugar and keep stirring over a gentle fire until it is melted. Remove all the scum as it rises, and just before the jam is done, boil it rapidly for five minutes. To ascertain when it is sufficiently boiled, pour a little on a plate, and if the syrup thickens and appears firm, it is done. Have ready half the kernels blanched, put them into the jam give them one boil and pour the preserve into pots.

When cold cover down with oiled papers and over these tissue paper brushed with the white of an egg.

Time: three-quarters of an hour after the sugar is added.

Barley Water

1 teaspoonful barley
Thin rind and juice of one lemon
1 quart water, which must be boiling
Sugar to taste.

Summertime:
A posy of godetia, larkspur, schizanthus red
alyssum and grasses.

AUGUST

When the harvest home is borne

August bring the sheaves of corn

AUGUST

Then the harvest home is borne

August Flowers

	meaning
Fuchsia	Taste
Ox-eye daisy	A token
Mustard	Indifferent
Fennel	Worthy of all praises
Rosebay willow herb	Pretension
Codlins & Cream	Freedom
Tansy	I declare war against you
Petunia	Never despair
Mallow	Mildness
Black medick	Quiet meeting
Thistle	Austerity
Yarrow	Pure in heart
Melilot	An appointment
Sweet pea	Departure
Peony	Shame

Birthflower   Yarrow

Birthstone   Peridot. Said to give the wearer confidence.

Family sayings:

'As ye sow so shall ye reap'.

'If you sow the wind, reap the whirlwind'.

'He who would thrive must rise at five,
He who has thriven may lie till seven,
And he who by the plough would live
Himself must either lead or drive'.

Diary Notes for August

August 1st

The local farmers have been busy gathering the crops recently and now their next job is well underway: stubble burning. Although strictly controlled, I always feel a pang of regret when I see a field burning; regret for the wild life trapped by the smoke and unable to escape.

August 2nd

Father's greenhouse is bursting with hybrid fuchsia blooms. I am only interested in the more hardy red and blue varieties such as "Mrs Popple" and "Jack French", which grow outside in both gardens. In the greenhouse though, "Evensong", "Swingtime", and many others with fancy names reign supreme. I think Father always looks relieved when I leave his 'dancing ballerinas' in peace. He is convinced I shall invent a new method of pressing flowers which will make his prize blooms more attractive when pressed. Hybrid fuchsias are fleshy and the pale colours just turn to brown when pressed.

August 3rd

Holly and I took my Aunt's dog for a walk this evening. On the way home we saw a flock of geese on the wing. What a beautiful picture they made as they flew into the sunset past fields of golden corn.

August 4th, Exmouth

We are taking a short holiday in Devon to relax and enjoy a few clotted cream teas. However, I shall be attending one crafts fair in Exmouth tomorrow. This has been a tradition of mine over the past couple of years. I am looking forward to meeting up with old friends and making a few new ones too.

The gardens here are alight with hydrangeas of every colour and hue, pretty fuchsias, ox-eye daisies and many other garden flowers. The countryside is typically August though, very dried up. But, I did see a beautiful wild carrot plant in full bloom when we were touring around this evening.

August 5th

I have been busy at the Crafts Fair all day – catching up on the news mainly! My stand is opposite to a lady who paints on ivory. Her family used to make church organs – and she is now using up the left over pieces of keys to base her miniatures on. I thought they were fascinating and Peter very kindly bought me a tiny picture of a bluebird – which I shall treasure.

August 10th

We arrived home today but Peter decided to take the whole family out to Sunday lunch with a difference. We all drove to Loughborough and boarded the "Carillion" for lunch along the Great Central Railway. Holly was mesmerised by the steam train which chuffed slowly along to Swithland Reservoir where it stopped so that the passengers could admire the view – and most important – eat a beautifully-cooked lunch. The day was cool and a light drizzle made swirls in the water. The ducks were quite happy though and swam, and dipped, and quacked, as usual.

The railway banks were still very colourful. Mustard, fennel, rosebay willow herb and the more usual thickets of bramble and wild raspberry can bloom here undisturbed. The railway banks are of course a haven for butterflies, bees and various larger forms of wild life. The butterfly population has undergone a great decline in recent years, but I was pleased to see, even in such poor weather conditions, many types flitting from flower to flower.

August 16th

There are many cotton thistles about now. In addition to being a very imposing flowering plant, the stems may be boiled then eaten with butter. In the sixteen hundreds the cotton fibres of the plant were collected and used as the stuffing for pillows.

August 17th

The swallows are gathering on the telephone wires outside our house, chattering noisily. They are getting ready for their long, long flight to warmer climes. Migration is extremely dangerous for them and other wild birds too. Many are eaten by predators and even more end up in butchers' shops across the Continent. Not surprisingly, the numbers of migrating birds have dwindled over the years.

August 18th

This is the time of year to gather petals for pot pourri, lavender for lavender bags and everlasting flowers for those Winter arrangements.

August 23rd, Town and Country Show, Stoneleigh

This show is rather spectacular, and should not be missed during the August Bank Holiday. There is always a large Crafts section, housed in freshly painted sheds which sometimes also contain the odd cow, sheep or caged bird! Dad always takes a good deal of trouble to erect our stand at this event. Usually we build up our display over two days.

August 25th

The last day of the show has been spoilt by heavy rain and strong gales of wind attributed to Hurricane Charley, which has wrought havoc in North America before turning its attention to us. The show was over long before the official finish at 7.30 p.m. Father took charge of Holly and the stock of unsold goods leaving Delphine and me to trudge through the driving rain to the car park. I was carrying a white folding table and managed to trip over a tent peg, fall — then slide along in the mud using the table as a low-level skate-board.

At the main gate a policeman stopped the traffic so that I could squelch my way over to the car park with the minimum of fuss. We arrived home to find the patio chairs strewn across the lawn, panes of glass lost from the greenhouse once again, and most of the apple crop on the lawn. Now I know what is meant by the saying 'One of those days'.

August 30th

I heard on the News that this has been a record year for Red Kite fledglings. This very rare bird lives mostly in hilly areas in Wales and its numbers have been on the decline for over two hundred years. The Kite builds its bulky nest from twigs and sticks bound together with mud, and lined with either moss, wool, hair and in some instances paper and linen. "When the Kite builds look to lesser linen" wrote Shakespeare.

Seven nests had been raided for their eggs this year, but despite this thirty-eight fledglings have been reared.

August Recipes

Pot Pourri – My mother's recipe.

Pick from the garden a good quantity of:

Rose petals (pulled gently from the flower head – blemish free petals are best!)

Rose geranium leaves, lavender flowers, elderflowers, cornflower florets, marigold petals.

Take all indoors and spread variety by variety onto absorbent tissue or fabric placed on trays. Leave to dry in a warm airy place for about three weeks.

To make Pot Pourri the following are also required:

2 tablespoons ground, dried orange peel
2 teaspoons freshly ground cloves
2 teaspoons freshly ground allspice
2 teaspoons ground cardamon seeds
2 tablespoons orris root powder
1 teaspoon rose oil
½ teaspooon sandalwood oil
3 drops lavender oil

Mode:

Mix together the spices and add
5 cups rose petals
3 cups rose geranium leaves
1 cup lavender flowers
1 cup elderflowers
1 cup marigold petals
1 cup cornflower florets

Statice and other everlasting flowers may also be added to give more colour.

Mix all dry ingredients in a large basin adding the oil and orris root powder last. Cover with cling film and leave to mature for two or three weeks. Inspect and stir mixture from time to time. When pot pourri has matured, transfer to pretty bowls and distribute around the house. More oils can be added drop by drop to freshen up when the fragrance dwindles.

Warm September brings the fruit

SEPTEMBER

Sportsmen then begin to shoot

SEPTEMBER
A circle of hydrangea for the season
of mists and mellow fruitfulness

September Flowers

	meaning
Bindweed	Insinuation
Bugdelia	Let me go
Convolvulus (Morning glory)	Extinguished hopes
Feverfew	Pretty maiden
Gladiolus	Strength of character
Hydrangea	Boastful
Ivy leaved toadflax	Domestic industry
Michaelmas daisy	Afterthought
Lady's mantle	Celestial
Red and white dead-nettle	Slander
Sorrel	Affection

Birthflower   Gladiolus

Birthstone   Sapphire. Worn to protect the owner from harm.
The blue stone represents purity of soul.

September sayings:

'Trust not a man who has no friendship for flowers'.

Ode to American tourists:
'It only rains here in September
April throu' June to dull November.
Visiting us?
The Winter's best
Then it snows
And gives the rain a rest!'.

Diary Notes for September

September 6th

I awoke this morning to greet the first misty morn of Autumn. A beautiful mellow day followed, the sun shining brightly once the mist had cleared. I took Fergie, my Aunt's little dog for a long walk in the country. How he enjoyed gambolling through the thickets, chasing imaginary rabbits, dead leaves, and failing all else – his tail! Some of the trees are showing the first gold threads of Autumn. The hedgerows glisten with berries of all description. Holly loves blackberries though I always make her wash them before eating.

September 7th

Visited my Father-in-law at his charming cottage in Sibbertoft, and spent a happy hour pottering in his garden gathering plant material for my flower presses. The cottage is very old and whoever lived there in times gone-by must have been a keen amateur herbalist, for the garden is ablaze with:

Tanzy	*used for*	mouthwashes
Feverfew		curing complaints connected with childbirth 'It does a woman all the good she can desire of a herb' said Culpepper.
Lady's mantle		muscle growth
Ox-eye daisy		eye disease/liver complaints
Clary		eye disease

September 8th

It is much cooler today. Doreen, Dad's neighbour said there had been a ground frost for the last three mornings.

The housemartins must have flown with the rising sun for their nesting site is quite empty and my upstairs workshop is quiet without their chatter.

This evening I visited my neighbour who is in hospital. Driving to Northampton I noticed some beautiful red leaves in the hedgerows. If the weather is fine tomorrow I shall gather some for my press.

Early Autumn:
The flowers for this picture are fuchsias,
pansies, larkspur, potentilla and astrantia.

September 9th

Picked hydrangea for my press, it's a lovely dark pink colour. Later on the petals turn deep red and look well on Winter pictures. It is said: to turn pink hydrangea to blue, place rusty nails in the soil below the roots.

September 10th

My birthday. 'Wednesday's child is full of woe'. I wonder if the family think the saying is true of me.

September 13th

'Windy night
Rainy morrow'.
Torrential rain dashed the leaves from the trees this evening helped along by the howling wind.

September 19th

Recorded temperatures of over 70 degrees F. today quite a little heatwave. The Bugdelia plant in our front garden is in full bloom and alive with bees and butterflies of all description. The 'Indian Summer' has caused a great revival of the garden flowers but the hedgerows are beginning to look rather bedraggled. The sorrel plants are beautiful at this time of the year though, their stems, leaves, and fruits splashed with red.

Much wild foliage is dying away leaving that other awesome "crop" the litter of civilised man. We have a golden harvest of drink cans, broken glass, garden refuse and even an old mattress adorning the verges near the village.

September 23rd

The first day of Autumn today — the season of 'mists and mellow fruitfulness'. A pleasant rather warm start to the season.

September 27th

A large parcel of heather arrived from Scotland from Uncle Fred so I was kept busy pressing the florets before they became too dry. Heather has always been a useful plant for man being gathered as a form of fuel in early times. Centuries later it was used for making brushes and brooms and thatching material, and for lining the walls of wee crofts in the Highlands of Scotland.

September 29th, Michaelmas Day

Dad has large clumps of michaelmas daisies of every shade and hue growing in his garden. These flowers are really a member of the aster family and originally came from North America. They were given the name 'michaelmas daisy' because they are in full bloom on Michaelmas Day and the flowers have yellow centres just like the common daisy.

September Recipes

Crab Apple Jelly. Grandma's recipe book

    1½lbs crab apples

    1 pint water

    10oz sugar to each lb of jam.

Method:

Take off the stalks, weigh and wash the crab apples, put them into a preserving pan and add the water. Boil gently until they are broken but they must not be allowed to fall to a pulp. Strain through a jelly bag and when the juice is transparent, weigh it, put it into a clean pan and boil it quickly for ten minutes, then take it off the fire and add the sugar. Stir until it is quite dissolved, place pan on the fire again and boil from twelve to fifteen minutes.

Pour into prepared pots and when cold cover down with oiled papers and over these tissue paper brushed over with the white of an egg.

Blackberry wine – Great Grandmother's recipe

To each quart of fruit add one quart of cold water. Put in a jug and stir every day for twelve days, then sieve it and add one pound of sugar to every quart of wine. Add a little grated ginger.

Put in a warm corner to work and skim every other day for sixteen days then bottle. Put a little sugar at the bottom of the bottles before putting the wine in. Leave the corks slack until the wine has finished working.

Autumn:
The golden time of year. The flowers in the
picture are autumn pansies, feverfew,
potentilla (Red Ace), montbretia, nemesia
and astrantia. I have added seed pods and
red leaves for effect.

Fresh October brings the pheasant

OCTOBER

Then to gather nuts is pleasant

OCTOBER
The potentilla bloom on

October Flowers

	meaning
Dahlia, single	Good taste
Dahlia, double	Instability
Marigold	Jealousy
Golden rod	Precaution
Mesembryanthemum	Idleness
Autumn crocus	Mirth
Potentilla	Maternal affection

Birthflower	Single dahlia

Birthstone	Opal. The symbol of hope. It is thought to protect the wearer from poisoning and help to maintain a good memory.

Family sayings:

'The World is full of such wonderful things
Why! We should all be as happy as Kings'.

'If foxes bark in the fields in October
Deep snow will cover their tracks all the Winter'.

Diary Notes for October

October 2nd

The weather continues to be unseasonally warm and I now have a second crop of dog roses on one of the bushes in the garden. I have also been busy picking daisies, potentilla and fuchsias for my flower presses.

October 4th

Dad Draper reports that the swallows have finally vacated the nest underneath the eaves of his cottage, so we must expect the fine weather to end soon.

October 5th

Harvest Festival Sunday for Welford Church. The church looked really beautiful with decorations of fruit, vegetables and flowers. The children took a Harvest offering of vegetables to the Family Service at 10 a.m. Holly enjoyed taking her little parcel of gifts to the church and placing it on the gifts table. The produce is later collected by the village schoolchildren and distributed to the senior citizens in the community.

The swallows flew away too soon for the weather continues to be sunny and rather mild for the time of year. This afternoon I picked even more pansies, violas, larkspur and even buttercups, all from my garden.

October 11th

A sharp frost this morning followed by a beautiful sunny day.

October 18th

On my way home from a Crafts show this evening I saw a fox – he had obviously escaped the Hunt which meets around here most weekends.

October 21st

Holly and I have been making up lavender bags for the linen cupboard. The custom of scenting sheets with herbs was introduced to this country by the Romans.

October 28th

Hallow'een Night of 'Ghoulies, Ghosties and Long-legged Beasties'. We do not celebrate this festival in this part of the country – though we occasionally have some young callers dressed up for 'trick or treat'. My Father's family were of Scots descent though, so we have a rather interesting collection of family superstitions.

Family Superstitions

Never put up a fence between neighbours because the fence soon becomes a wall of silence.

Do not burn bread or scraps on the fire – it feeds the Devil.

Always give a penny in return for scissors, razors, a manicure set, otherwise it cuts a friendship.

Never give gloves as a gift – an argument will follow.

If a bird taps on the window there will be a death in the family.

A calendar or picture falling off the wall is also a sign of a death in the family.

A magpie in the garden is very unlucky unless it has a mate.

A robin in the garden is also unlucky, especially in the Summer.

The itch:

Left hand	–	Lose money
Right hand	–	A windfall
Nose itching	–	Kissed, cursed or vexed
Foot itching	–	Strange ground

If a child cuts front teeth which are parted – he or she will have far to travel in life.

Dream of the dead – hear from the living.

If the lid is left off the teapot after mashing a pot of tea unexpected visitors will arrive.

If a bumble bee flies into the house it is also a sign of unexpected visitors.

Harvest Vegetables and their meanings

	meaning
Apples	Temptation
Branch of currants	You please all
Bundle of reeds with their panicles	Music
Cabbage	Profit
Corn	Riches
Corn, broken	A quarrel
Corn straw	Agreement
Cranberry	Hardness
Cress	Stability
Dead leaves	Sadness
Figs	Argument
Hops	Injustice
Lettuce	Cold hearted
Lemon	Zest
Mint	Virtue
Oats	The witching sound of music
Peach	Your qualities like your charms
Pear	Affection
Pomegranite	Fool
Potato	Benevolence
Quince	Temptation
Raspberry	Remorse
Rhubarb	Advice
Turnip	Charity
Walnut	Strength
Wheat stalk	Riches

October Recipes

Potted Rabbit: Grandma's recipe

Boil a rabbit in very little water until tender. When cooked rub through a sieve. Put rabbit in a saucepan and add six ounces butter and a little of the liquor that it was boiled in. Season to taste. Cook gently for one hour. Put into moulds. When cooled pour melted butter on top, six cloves, and six peppercorns. For a richer flavour put a little black mace into the saucepan when the rabbit is cooked for the first time.

Pickled Walnuts: Aunt Nan's recipe book

100 walnuts, salt, and water.

To each quart of vinegar allow 2oz. black peppers, 2oz allspice and 1oz bruised ginger.

The walnuts should be young and not woody. Prick them with a fork. Put them into a brine strong enough to float an egg, letting them remain nine days. Change the brine twice during this time. Drain them off. (Put on a large dish to drain.) Dry. Place in the sun until they become perfectly black which will be in two or three days. Place the walnuts in dry jars. Boil vinegar for ten minutes with the spices in above proportion and pour it over the walnuts while hot. The walnuts must be covered with the liquid. Tie down and keep in a dry place.

NOVEMBER

A cheerful arrangement using winter hydrangea

Dull November brings the blast

NOVEMBER

Then the leaves are whirling fast

November Flowers

	meaning
Chrysanthemum, white	Truthful
Chrysanthemum, yellow	Slighted love
Chrysanthemum, red	I love you
Azalea	Temperance
Cyclamen	Diffidence

Birthflower	Chrysanthemum, white

Birthstone	Topaz: which means fire. It protects wearer from asthma and ensures sound slumber.

The language of trees:

	meaning
Ash	Grandure
Aspen	Lamentation
Bay Tree	Glory
Beech tree	Prosperity
Box	Stoicism
Bramble	Remorse
Cherry	Good education
Chestnut	Luxury
Dogwood	Durability
Elm	Dignity
Fig	Prolific
Laurel	Ambition
Lime	Love
Oak	Hospitality
Palm	Victory
Poplar	Time
Weeping willow	Mourning

Family Lullaby:

'Go to sleep my baby
Close your pretty eyes
Wake up in the morning
When the sun is in the sky'.

Diary Notes for November

November 1st

The 'back end of the year' is with us again. This is an especially busy time for the gardener. I have been out planting daffodils, tulips, narcissus, snowdrops and many more traditional spring-flowering bulbs. I shall now keep my fingers crossed that they all bloom.

November 5th – Guy Fawkes Night

Holly had a bonfire party. She likes the roast potatoes and the pretty fireworks and rockets – but the loud banging varieties were enjoyed more by her Grandfathers and her Daddy.

November 9th, Rememberance Sunday

The symbol is the red poppy immortalised in a poem by Colonel John McCrae entitled 'In Flanders Fields'. In the language of flowers the red poppy means consolation.

November 10th

A fairly warm day in all. The leaves are indeed falling fast from the trees. Out walking today I saw that the hedgerows are still ablaze with hips and haws. The birds must be saving them up for more wintry days. I also spied a small grey squirrel gathering a few more stores for the Winter. It was a sad day when this pest was introduced to Britain from America. It has taken over from the more enchanting red squirrel and also has a nasty habit of eating the bark from trees – making it unpopular with farmer and forester alike.

November 28th

For the last few years Delphine and I have started a new family tradition of making Christmas puddings and cake, on this day. We all make a wish in the Christmas pudding. It's one way of getting the mixture thoroughly stirred!

November 29th

It has rained all day but I have a delightful cyclamen in flower in the kitchen which has helped to brighten up a dreary day. In years gone by the cyclamen corms were used as fodder for pigs. In the sixteenth century the tuberous roots were also much sought after as a remedy for baldness. Small pieces of the root were gathered and placed up the nose!

November 30th, St. Andrew's Day

The emblem of Scotland is the thistle.

November Recipes

Christmas Pudding. Mother's recipe.

8oz SR flour
1lb fresh white breadcrumbs
1lb brown sugar
1lb chopped suet
1lb currants
1lb raisins
1lb sultanas
8oz mixed peel
2oz ground almonds
8 eggs
Rind of one lemon finely grated
2 teaspoons almond essence
1 teaspoon ground ginger
1 teaspoon mixed spice
1 teaspoon cinnamon
Pinch salt
Pinch nutmeg
1 pint flat stout

Look over the dried fruit and take out any stalks or pips left behind. Mix all the fruit together in a large basin.

In a separate bowl mix the flour, breadcrumbs, brown sugar, and spices. Transfer these ingredients to the basin containing the fruit and bind altogether with the eggs and half a pint of flat stout. The mixture will not take all the liquor so this should be added after the mixture has settled, usually overnight.

The next day divide the mixture between two or three lightly greased pudding basins. Cover each with a round of greaseproof paper and make a tin foil lid over the top. Boil for seven hours making sure the saucepan does not boil dry. The puddings will need a further two hours on Christmas Day.

Horseradish vinegar. Aunt Drue's recipe.

      ¼lb scraped horseradish
      1oz minced shalot
      1 drachm of cayenne
      1 quart of vinegar

Put all the ingredients into a bottle, which shake well from time to time for a fortnight. When it is thoroughly steeped, strain and bottle. It will be ready for use immediately. This will be found an agreeable relish to cold beef. This vinegar should be made either in October or November as horseradish is then in its highest perfection.

Great Grandma's golden rules for Bread making.

(reproduced exactly as written in her recipe book)

"To make good home made bread"

1 quartern of flour, 1 large tablespoonful of solid brewer's yeast, or nearly 1 ounce of fresh German yeast, 1¼ to 1½ pints of warm milk and water.

Mode:

Put the flour into a large earthenware bowl or deep pan, then with a strong metal or wooden spoon, hollow out the middle; but do not clear it entirely away from the bottom of the pan, so in that case, the sponge or leaven (as it was formally termed) would stick to it, which it ought not to do. Next, take either a large tablespoonful of yeast which has now been rendered solid by mixing it with plenty of cold water, and letting it afterwards stand to settle for a day and a night, or nearly an ounce of German yeast. Put it into a large basin and proceed to mix it so that it shall be as smooth as cream, with ¾ pint of warm milk and water, or with water only, though even a little milk will improve the bread. Pour the yeast into the hole made in the flour and stir into it as much of that which lies round it as will make a thick batter, in which, there must be no lumps. Strew plenty of flour on the top. Throw a thick clean cloth over it, and set it where the air is warm. Do not place it on the kitchen fender, for it will become so much heated there. Look at it from time to time, when it has been laid for nearly an hour, and when the yeast is risen and broken through the flour, so that bubbles appear in it, you will know that it is ready to be made up into dough.

Place the pan on a chair, or table, pour into the sponge the remainder of the warm milk and water and stir into it as much of the flour as you can with a spoon. Then wipe it clean with your fingers and lay it aside. Next take plenty of flour, throw it on top of the leaven and begin kneading it well with both hands. When the flour is nearly all kneaded in, begin to draw the edges of the dough towards the middle, in order to mix it thoroughly. When it is free from flour and lumps and does not stick to the hands when touched, it will be done and may be covered with a cloth and left to rise a second time. In three-quarters of an hour look at it, it should have swollen very much and begin to crack and it will be light enough to bake.

Turn it onto a pasteboard and with a sharp knife divide it in two. Make it quickly into loaves and put it in the oven. Make a cross on top of the loaves as they will rise more easily if this is done. All bread should be turned upside-down as soon as it comes from the oven. If you do not do this the under part of the loaves will become wet and blistered from the steam which cannot escape from them.

Time to be left to rise: an hour the first time, three-quarters of an hour the second time. To be baked from 1 to 1¾ hours if baked in one loaf from 1½ to 2 hours.

Chill December brings the sleet

DECEMBER

Blazing fire, and Christmas treat

DECEMBER:
The very name of flowers bring
Spring to me in Winter's hours.

December Flowers

	meaning
Christmas rose	Relieve my anxiety
Helleborus	Scandal
Poinsettia	Joy

Birthflower	Christmas rose

Birthstone	Turquoise – much prized by the ancient Egyptians, it means 'constant love'.

Evergreens pretty in December:

	meaning
Holly	Foresight
Ivy	Glory
Laurel	Fidelity
Privet	Diffidence

Family sayings:

'Be thankful, my child and forget not to pray
Your thanks to that Father above,
Who gives you so many more blessings each day,
And crowns your whole life with his love'.

'Aye flowers! The very name of flowers,
That bloom in wood and glen,
Brings Spring to me in Winter's hours,
And childhood dreams again'.

'Give me sunshine, rhymes and reasons,
Laughter, and flowers for all seasons'.

Diary Notes for December

December 1st, Holly's birthday

December 10th

A sharp frost this morning, the first really hard one of the season. The air has been crisp and clear and the hedgerows covered in a lacy cloth of cob-webs, shimmering in the sunlight. Once the frost had evarporated I was amazed to find the fuchsias, potentilla, pansies, and tiny violets in the garden had not beeen affected.

December 16th

Spent the morning in the garden. The violets are sending out shoots and the daffodils and crocus bulbs are showing green tips. It is exceptionally mild today for the time of year.

December 21st

We awoke this morning to a white world filled with swirling snow. It is time to put away the flower presses until next year and declare the Christmas season open.

This afternoon Holly and I put up the decorations although we will be spending the Christmas holiday at "My Way" with the family. Aunt Nan brought us some boughs of holly from her garden. We do not have any mistletoe as there is a national shortage. It is a good idea to save the berries after twelfth night and store them until Spring in a cool, dry place. By April the white berries will have rotted and the pips can be transferred to the underside of a branch of apple, lime, or poplar tree. Make a nick in the branch and place the seeds inside. Mistletoe will then be secured for future generations.

December 22nd

A gentle thaw this afternoon. It is the shortest day of the year and heralds the start of the Winter season.

December 24th, Christmas Eve

Holly and my Father collected the turkey from a local farm. Holly is convinced that Spring has come because the farmer was shearing sheep. He will keep them indoors over the next few weeks as early lambs are expected. The sheep would be far too warm in their thick coats.

December 25th, Christmas Day

A picture book day of frosty air and blue skies outside and log fires and Christmas treats inside. Holly thought Santa had been very kind to her by leaving so many presents under the tree.

The tradition of the Christmas tree was introduced to England by Prince Albert when he requested one for a children's party at Windsor Castle in 1841.

December 26th, Boxing Day

In the last century servants and trades people would receive presents of money or 'Christmas boxes' on this day which is how the name Boxing Day came about. It is also the feast day of St. Stephen.

December 27th

The Christmas roses are in bloom in Father's garden. They are really a member of the buttercup family and make a welcome splash of green against the cold brown earth.

December 31st

A dull day brightened up by the winter-flowering almond tree in my garden. The flowers mean "Hope of Spring". I feel rather sad because this is the last entry in my diary. Turning over the pages and reading what I have written a saying of my Mother's comes to mind:

> 'Let us all reflect with pleasure
> That labour is a source of treasure'.

It has been a joy rather than a labour to write about flowers for all seasons and I hope that you have enjoyed reading about them.

Christmas Treats

Toffee. Mum's recipe.

> 1lb Demerara sugar
> 6oz butter
> Small cup of water
> 4 tablespoons of vinegar
> A little essence of lemon

Boil gently for half an hour. Move mixture around by moving the pan but do not stir with a spoon. Place a few drops in a glass of water. If they set the mixture is ready.

Turkish Delight. Grandma's recipe.

Boil three lbs loaf sugar in a copper pan with two pints of cold water. As soon as this boils and becomes clear — dissolve 4½oz of starch in a little water and add it to the sugar, gradually stirring all the while. Keep stirring until the syrup becomes a thick paste then add half-a-cupful of hot water with a cupful of sweet blanched almonds chopped into small pieces. Flavour with essence of vanilla or lemon. Pour the mixture onto a greased slab. When cold cut it into squares and dip into powdered sugar.

Honey Fudge, my recipe.

> 4oz honey
> 1lb granulated sugar
> 3 teaspoons water
> ⅛ teaspoon cream of tartar
> 2 egg whites beaten until stiff
> ½ teaspoon vanilla essence
> ½ teaspoon desiccated coconut

Method:

Place in a saucepan honey, sugar, water, cream of tartar and bring slowly to the boil until a temperature of 260F is reached. Pour the boiling syrup onto the egg white beating all the time. Add vanilla essence and coconut. Beat mixture until thick and creamy, pour into a greased pan and leave to set overnight. Cut into squares the next day — but leave exposed to the air for a further two days so that the mixture hardens.

Early Winter:
The flowers include potentilla, hydrangea,
polyanthus and the last of the candytuft.

Christmas Cake

Great Grandma's recipe.

8oz butter

8oz soft brown sugar

6 eggs

9oz self-raising flour *

5oz plain flour

pinch salt

½ teaspoon mixed spice

2oz ground almonds

2oz peel

2lbs mixed fruit

4oz glace cherries

A little lemon juice

Tablespoon of black treacle

Wine

* I have changed this from 'flour' and omitted baking powder.

Mode:

Look over fruit and take out any stalks and seeds. Mix fruit, cherries, lemon juice, and mixed peel with enough sherry or wine to cover. Leave for one week stirring every day.

Cream together butter and sugar. Whisk egg yolks and add to mixture. Sieve together the flour, ground almonds, salt and spices and add to the mixture with the whites of the eggs whisked until stiff. Add the fruit and any wine juice. A little black treacle may be added with a little gravy browning to darken the mixture.

Bake in a moderate oven for four hours.

To everything there is a purpose
And a time to every Season under heaven.

The Spirit of Winter

O come to the window, my children, and see
What a change there has been in the night.
The snow has quite covered the broad apple tree
And the garden is sprinkled with white.

The spring in the grove is beginning to freeze
The fish-pond is frozen all o'er;
Long icicles hang in bright rows from the trees,
And drop in odd shapes from the door.

The old mossy thatch and the meadow so green
Are hid with a mantle of white;
The snowdrop and crocus no longer are seen,
The thick snow has covered them quite.

The spirit of Winter:
The red potentilla represent the warmth of
the fireside, whilst outside the honesty seed
pods rattle in the wind next to the first daisies
and the snowdrops bringing a hope of Spring.